Coding History

There have been some amazing discoveries in the history of software, the programs that tell computers how to work and what to do.

Email
Ray Tomlinson creates the first email program, for sending digital messages.

WordStar
Micropro releases the first word processor, letting people easily write on computers.

Computer virus
"Brain" is the first worldwide computer virus. It spreads across computers through floppy disks.

Social media
The world's first social media network is created. It is called SixDegrees.

1969 — **1971** — **1979** — **1984** — **1986** — **1992** — **2003** — **2014**

ARPANET
The first computer network is built, forming the basis of today's modern Internet.

 http://www.

MacPaint and MacWrite
Apple releases two programs with its Macintosh computer, to allow users to draw and write on their computers.

The Apple Lisa, released in 1983, was one of the first personal desktop computers.

Internet browser
Mosaic, the world's first Internet browser, is released.

HTML5
The original HTML code for the World Wide Web is updated to HTML5, making it easier for coders to use.

Things to find out:

DK findout!

Coding

Author: James Floyd Kelly

Senior editor Lizzie Davey
Designer Emma Hobson
Project editors Manisha Majithia, Ishani Nandi
Art editor Nehal Verma
Editorial assistants Sarah Foakes,
Charles Raspin
Design assistant Ala Uddin
Managing editors Laura Gilbert, Alka Thakur
Managing art editors Diane Peyton Jones,
Romi Chakraborthy
Pre-production producer Dragana Puvacic
Producer Isabell Schart
Art director Martin Wilson
Publisher Sarah Larter
Publishing director Sophie Mitchell
Educational consultant Jacqueline Harris

First published in Great Britain in 2017 by
Dorling Kindersley Limited
80 Strand, London, WC2R 0RL

Copyright © 2017 Dorling Kindersley Limited
A Penguin Random House Company
10 9 8 7 6 5 4 3 2
003–299020–Jul/2017

A CIP catalogue record for this book
is available from the British Library.
ISBN: 978-0-2412-8506-0

Printed and bound in China

A WORLD OF IDEAS:
SEE ALL THERE IS TO KNOW

www.dk.com

Contents

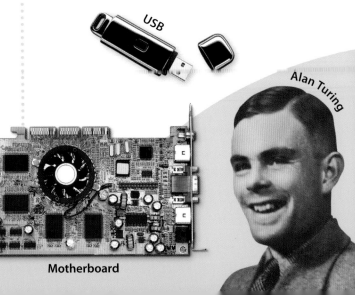

USB

Alan Turing

Motherboard

Mouse

Punched tape

Bugs

Apps

Graphic coding

The first computer

Robot

Floppy disk

3

What is a coder?

Coders, or programmers, are people who write the code for computer programs – a set of instructions that tell computers what to do. Many coders teach themselves how to code, others learn at school. Coders need a variety of different skills in order to build good programs.

Coders working together

Code in teams

While many coders work alone, most of them work in teams. Working in teams means programs are finished faster and with fewer errors. Teamwork also helps coders learn new skills from others.

Logical thinking

Computers follow rules and logic when running programs. Coders need to be able to think like a computer when writing code, and build in all the steps necessary for the program to work.

Many languages

Being able to code in different computer languages is a valuable skill. It is important for programmers to keep learning new coding languages in order to create modern programs.

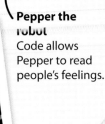

Pepper the robot
Code allows Pepper to read people's feelings.

Creating code
A typical coder's screen is filled with code like this.

Testing a new tablet

Staying up to date

Technology is constantly changing. Coders must stay up to date with the latest programming languages and techniques. This can help them find jobs and build programs for the latest devices.

Accuracy

Coders must always check and re-check code to make sure programs will work correctly. The instructions need to be clear, detailed, and broken down into small chunks that are easy to follow.

Coding in space

Space code
Astronaut and flight engineer Sunita Williams uses her laptop whilst in space.

How do you become a coder?

You're never too young to learn how to code. There are many books that teach coding, as well as plenty of information online. You can also learn to code at school, or you could find out if there are any coding clubs near you.

School kids coding

Micro:bit
Used in schools to teach coding.

Raspberry Pi
A mini-computer that shows people how computers work.

Codes around us

When we think of coding, we think of computers but codes are all around us. Throughout history, humans have created many different codes for communicating. Some codes are used to send secret messages, while others deliver information across long distances. People who cannot see or hear can use codes to speak to each other.

Blind people use their hands to read Braille.

Morse code

Morse code sent messages long distance along electric wires. Each letter was represented by a series of dots and dashes tapped out on a special machine.

A .-	M --	Y -.--
B -...	N -.	Z --..
C -.-.	O ---	1 .----
D -..	P .--.	2 ..---
E .	Q --.-	3 ...--
F ..-.	R .-.	4 ....-
G --.	S ...	5 .....
H	T -	6 -....
I ..	U ..-	7 --...
J .---	V ...-	8 ---..
K -.-	W .--	9 ----.
L .-..	X -..-	0 -----

This is a short sound, or a dot.

This is a long sound, or a dash.

Morse code tapping machine

WOW!

The **Ancient Egyptians** had more than **700 different hieroglyphs.**

Picture language

Ancient Egyptians didn't have an alphabet system. Instead, they used a series of pictures called hieroglyphs to represent sounds and words.

This stone is covered with hieroglyphs.

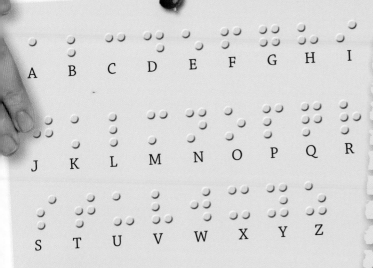

A B C D E F G H I

J K L M N O P Q R

S T U V W X Y Z

Braille
Some blind people use a system called Braille to read and write. Different sets of raised dots represent letters and numbers.

Semaphore flags
Semaphore is a system of signalling with hand-held flags. It is often used by ships at sea because the flags are easy to see from far away. The flags are held in different positions to signal letters and numbers.

1
2
3

4
5
6

7
8
9

This woman is learning sign language.

Sign language
As deaf people can't hear sounds, they can use sign language to communicate. Letters, numbers, and words can be shown using a variety of hand signs.

Coding before computers

Even before the invention of the modern computer, people were creating code. Many early programs took the form of cards punched with holes, which represented a set of instructions. These cards were read by machines to perform different tasks.

Pascaline

The Pascaline was invented by French mathematician Blaise Pascal. It was a simple calculating device that could add and subtract.

Sums were calculated by the movement of drums and gears inside the box.

Jacquard loom

This weaving machine was made by Joseph Jacquard. It could weave patterns in fabric by following instructions from cards punched with holes.

FACT FILE

» **When:** Early 1800s

» **Function:** Loom

» **Fun fact:** Fabric patterns today are still created using special computer programs.

Census machine

Herman Hollerith invented this machine to record data for the 1890 US census. It used punched cards to record information such as age and gender.

A clerk would sit at the desk and insert punched cards into the machine.

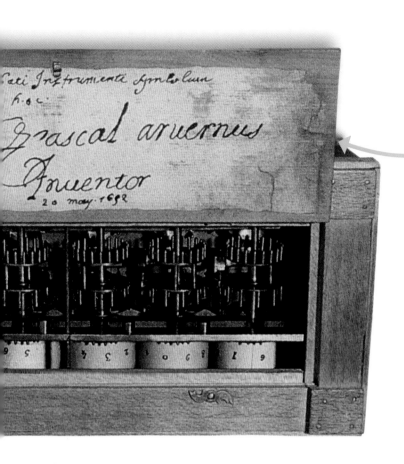

Each number was displayed in a box above its dial.

Numbers were entered by turning the dials.

FACT FILE

» **When:** 1642

» **Function:** Calculator

» **Fun fact:** Pascal was only 19 years old when he invented this machine.

FACT FILE

» **When:** 1890

» **Function:** Census data collection

» **Fun fact:** Hollerith's company later became the technology company IBM.

Player piano

From the 1850s, a number of pianos were invented that played themselves. They were called player pianos. Many used a paper music roll with holes to control which notes were played.

FACT FILE

» **When:** 19th century

» **Function:** Self-playing piano

» **Fun fact:** Sometimes called pianolas, player pianos are still used today.

The roll could be swapped to play different pieces of music.

The keys moved up and down when the piano was playing.

Coding pioneer

In 1842, English mathematician Ada Lovelace became the world's first computer programmer. She is best known for her work on an early mechanical computer made by Charles Babbage. She helped to pave the way for the future of computers. This is an imaginary conversation with the clever countess.

FACT FILE

» **Name:** Augusta Ada King-Noel, Countess of Lovelace

» **Dates:** 1815–52

» **Location:** England

» **Fun fact:** When Ada was 12 years old, she tried to build a flying machine!

Q: Ada, when did you find out you were good at maths?

A: Very early on. Even as a child I remember being good at solving mathematical problems.

Q: Do you come from a family of mathematical geniuses?

A: Not at all! However, my father was the celebrated poet, Lord Byron. I had tutors to teach me science and mathematics and although it was unusual for a young girl to learn these subjects, I soon found I was good at them.

Q: How did you meet computer genius Charles Babbage?

A: I was lucky enough to meet him in 1833 while he was teaching at Cambridge University in England.

Watercolour portrait of Ada from 1840

He showed me a version of his machine called the Difference Engine. It was designed to stop people getting maths calculations wrong.

Q: Is it right that Charles has given you a nickname?

A: Yes! Charles calls me the "Enchantress of Numbers" and he is called the "Father of Computing".

Q: Tell us about the machine that you worked on with Charles.

A: The Analytical Engine was the second machine designed by Charles, and it was fascinating! Charles gave me the designs for the machine. I realized that it could use codes made up of letters, symbols, and numbers to solve problems. It was the first computer that could be programmed.

Q: When did you actually write your computer program?

A: In 1842, I wrote a set of instructions and showed they could be used by the computer to solve a mathematics problem. A science journal in England published my findings.

Q: So you are the first computer programmer?

A: Well, yes, but I don't like to brag! What excites me most is this machine's potential. It is more than a calculator. The possibilities are endless! I believe all types of different things can be converted into computer code. Who knows what the future of computer coding will bring!

The Analytical Engine (1837) was designed by Charles Babbage to solve more complex maths calculations than ever before.

Modern-day laptop computer

Visionary
Ada Lovelace believed computers could one day be used to create music or art.

Top secret

The word "code" refers to a set of rules. Coders use these rules to tell computers what to do. However, codes can also be used to keep secrets. Throughout history, people have created codes to hide what a message says. A coded message can only be read if you know the secret rules to decode it.

Hail, Caesar!

Julius Caesar's code was very simple, but it worked for centuries. Most of his enemies could not read very well, so they thought he was writing his messages in a foreign language.

Polybius Square

The Greek historian Polybius worked for the Romans. He created a new code for their armies, using a square grid which matched each letter in the Greek alphabet to a pair of numbers. People with the same square could exchange messages written only in numbers.

Scytale

The Ancient Greeks of Sparta would scramble their messages by writing them on leather or parchment wrapped around a rod or stick. Then they added extra letters, so when the message was unwrapped from the rod it became a meaningless jumble.

Caesar shift

The Roman general and emperor Julius Caesar swapped each letter in his secret messages with a different one. Every letter moved a set number of spaces forwards in the alphabet, so in a one-shift code, "A" would become "B".

Alberti formula

In 1467, the Italian architect Leon Alberti invented a disc with two wheels, which could be rotated to swap one letter in a message for another. To swap the letters back and decode the message, you needed to know how the two discs had been rotated.

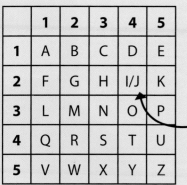

	1	2	3	4	5
1	A	B	C	D	E
2	F	G	H	I/J	K
3	L	M	N	O	P
4	Q	R	S	T	U
5	V	W	X	Y	Z

The Greek alphabet had only 24 letters.

The English grid puts I and J in the same square.

	1	2	3	4	5
1	Α	Β	Γ	Δ	Ε
2	Ζ	Η	Θ	Ι	Κ
3	Λ	Μ	Ν	Ξ	Ο
4	Π	Ρ	Σ	Τ	Υ
5	Φ	Χ	Ψ	Ω	

How it works

Find the letter you want to encode. Then, join the number above it and the number to the left of it. On the grid here, A is 11, while CAR is 31, 11, 24.

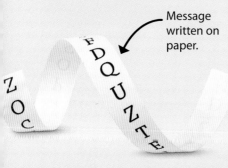

Message written on paper.

Paper wrapped around rod to reveal message.

How it works

The letters of the message only lined up correctly if the reader wrapped the strip of paper around a rod the same size as the one used to create it.

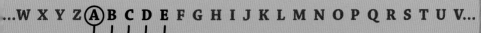

...W X Y Z (A) B C D E F G H I J K L M N O P Q R S T U V...

...W X (Y) Z A B C D E F G H I J K L M N O P Q R S T U V...

How it works

To decode a two-shift Caesar shift, move each letter in your message two spaces back in the alphabet. DCA would become BAY. Check the two rows on the left for examples.

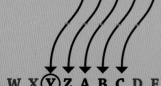

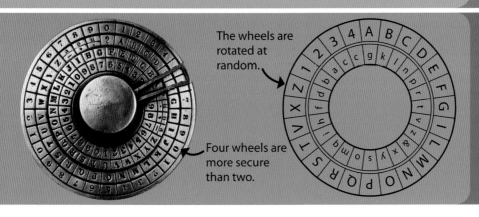

The wheels are rotated at random.

Four wheels are more secure than two.

How it works

Find each letter, number, or symbol you need on the inner wheel, and replace it with the matching letter on the outer wheel. The wheels must be in the same position to decode the message.

The Enigma code

In the 1930s, Germany wanted to control other countries. In 1939, it invaded Poland. Britain and France declared war in response, and World War II began. The war was fought with new technology like tanks, radar, and the top-secret Enigma machine.

Enigma machine

In World War II, armies fought on land, air, and sea, and moved between battles quickly. Telegraph and radio were used to send orders across huge distances.

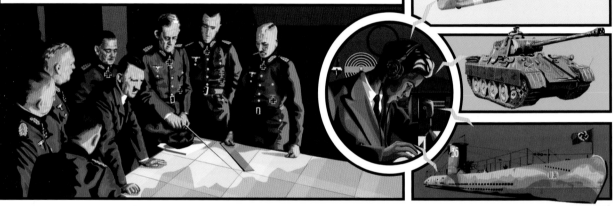

The Germans used a machine called Enigma to encode their messages. This allowed them to surprise their enemies, and communicate with their spies.

These secret orders made it impossible to track down the deadly German submarines, called U-boats.

In Britain, more than 10,000 people worked to break the Enigma code at a top-secret base called Bletchley Park, or "Station X".

Some of the world's first computers were used at Bletchley Park, designed by top scientists and engineers like Alan Turing.

On 30 October 1942, three British sailors rescued a working Enigma machine from a sinking German U-boat.

We got the codes!

These machines helped Britain break Enigma, and control the sea.

Hurrah!

Victory!

Germany's control of the sea was broken. On 7 May 1945, Germany surrendered.

Alan Turing

Englishman Alan Turing was a maths and science genius. When World War II started, he joined Bletchley Park, a top-secret base, where he worked to break enemy codes and uncover Germany's plans. His inventions and ideas began the age of modern computers.

Each Bombe was 2 m (7 ft) wide, and weighed 0.9 tonnes (1 ton).

Secret work

Turing's work on codes and computing was so secret that few people were allowed to know about it, even after the war ended. Today, he is recognized as "the father of computing".

Turing machine

In 1936, Turing wrote about an imaginary machine that could perform any task, if it was given the right set of instructions. He never built one, but we call the idea a Turing machine.

Hidden voices

In 1944, Turing helped develop SIGSALY, a secure way of encrypting radio messages using random noise. It was also called the Green Hornet, because anyone listening in would only hear buzzing.

Bombe machine

In 1939, Turing designed the Bombe. This early computer cracked enemy codes by testing every possible combination the Enigma machine could use. Over 200 ran day and night at Bletchley Park

Turing test

In 1950, Turing imagined a test to decide if a computer was "intelligent". A human would communicate with a hidden partner and try to decide if they were really human, or a computer.

Tiger stripes

After the war, Turing used maths to explore new kinds of science. In 1951, he created an equation to explain how patterns form in living creatures, like stripes on tigers, or the number of fingers on a hand.

Computer chess

Turing published the world's first chess-playing program, *Turochamp*, in 1951. No computer had enough power to run it, so Turing used the program's rules to decide his moves in a real chess game.

The first computer

In 1943, engineers in the USA began designing a machine that could be programmed to solve different maths problems. This was the Electronic Numerical Integrator And Computer (ENIAC, "en-ee-ack") – the first computer. The ENIAC could follow 5,000 instructions per second, which was 1,000 times faster than the calculators of the time. It was huge and filled a whole room.

The **ENIAC** weighed **27 tonnes** (30 tons) – the same as **five elephants**.

How it worked

The ENIAC did not have "insides" as modern computers do. Instead, its parts were fixed to 40 panels. Each panel had hundreds of wires, switches, and tubes attached to it.

The ENIAC had more than 17,000 vacuum tubes

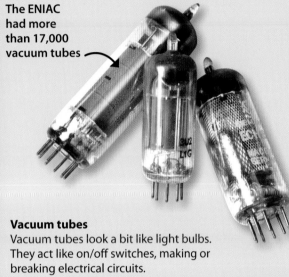

Vacuum tubes
Vacuum tubes look a bit like light bulbs. They act like on/off switches, making or breaking electrical circuits.

Men and women worked side by side to program the ENIAC.

Programming the ENIAC
Each time the ENIAC was programmed, everything had to be moved around by hand. Setting it up to perform a single task could take weeks.

Multi-tasking machines

The more tasks a computer can handle at once, the faster it can complete them all. The first computers could only handle one task, but these days a laptop or mobile phone can perform thousands of separate tasks, called processes, at the same time.

Z3

The Z3, built in Germany, was the world's first programmable computer. Older computers needed to be rewired to run new programs, but the Z3 stored its programs on paper tape. It was destroyed by bombs during World War II.

FACT FILE

» **When:** 1941

» **Weight:** 0.9 tonnes (1 ton)

» **Fun fact:** The German government refused to help improve the Z3. They felt computers were not important to the war.

SSEM

The Small-Scale Experimental Machine (SSEM) was built at Manchester University, UK. It was the first computer to store programs on its own memory, instead of on tape.

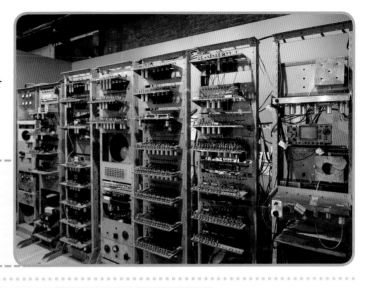

FACT FILE

» **When:** 1948

» **Weight:** 1 tonne (1.1 tons)

» **Fun fact:** The SSEM was nicknamed "Baby" as a joke, because it was so large.

UNIVAC I

The UNIVAC I was the first computer to be sold to the public in the USA. Its name stood for "Universal Automatic Computer". The UNIVAC I's memory used seven large tanks of liquid mercury, which picked up electrical signals from pulses of sound sent by quartz crystals.

FACT FILE

» **When:** 1951

» **Weight:** 13 tonnes (14.3 tons)

» **Fun fact:** UNIVAC I forecast Eisenhower's victory in the 1952 US presidential election before anyone else.

IBM System/360

The IBM 360 was the first series of computers to use programs that worked on more than one machine. They were designed to be affordable, so businesses could buy or rent them.

FACT FILE

» **When:** 1964

» **Weight:** Varied from 0.7 tonnes (0.75 tons) to 2.3 tonnes (2.6 tons)

» **Fun fact:** IBM 360 computers were used to plan the Apollo moon landings.

Think like a computer

Computers cannot think for themselves. They follow very specific instructions given by programmers. These instructions must be exact but simple. Programmers often break down complex instructions into smaller steps that are easier to follow.

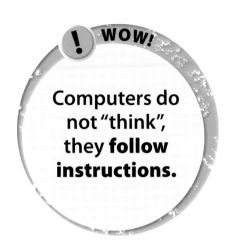

! WOW!

Computers do not "think", they **follow instructions.**

Follow the rules

This robot must get across the maze, following set steps like a computer does. It must follow the rules below. The algorithm has the same information as the rules, but written so that a computer (the robot) can follow them.

Each time the robot hits an obstacle, it follows the rules again, starting at the beginning of the algorithm.

Rules

» The robot is trying to get through the maze.

» The maze is filled with red doors, blue doors, and green doors.

» Red doors and blue doors should be ignored.

» Go through green doors.

» When a wall is encountered, try turning left or right.

Algorithm

START

Move forward

If stopped by wall
Turn right if no wall on right.
Turn left if no wall on left.
Go to START.

If red door is seen
Ignore.
Go to START.

If blue door is seen
Ignore.
Go to START.

If green door is seen
Open door.
Move into space beyond green door.
Close green door.
Go to START.

What is an algorithm?

Coders often develop a set of steps or instructions called an algorithm before they write any code. For example, programming a robot to put on a pair of socks might follow this simple algorithm.

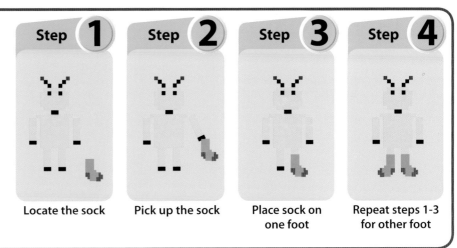

Step 1 — Locate the sock

Step 2 — Pick up the sock

Step 3 — Place sock on one foot

Step 4 — Repeat steps 1-3 for other foot

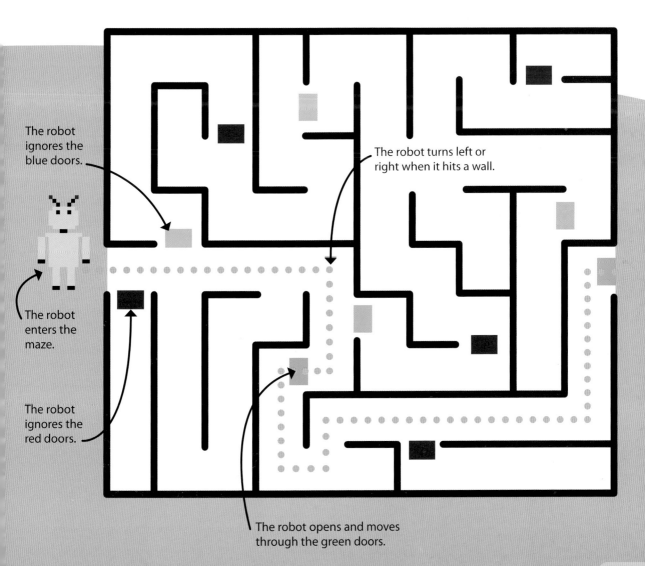

The robot ignores the blue doors.

The robot turns left or right when it hits a wall.

The robot enters the maze.

The robot ignores the red doors.

The robot opens and moves through the green doors.

Early games

Coders have been making games since the early days of computing. All the games we play need code, whether played on a computer, a television, or a mobile phone. These images look simple now, but when they were created they were groundbreaking!

PONG

Pong was created in 1972 by Atari. Two players used paddles with rotating knobs to bounce a "ball" back and forth. A point was scored when the other player missed the ball. There were two versions: an arcade game and one that attached to a television.

Atari 2600

The Atari 2600 was one of the earliest and most popular gaming systems sold for home use, from 1977. Games were small, rectangular plastic boxes that slotted into the box, called a console. The controls had joysticks for movement and a single "fire" button.

SPACE INVADERS

One of the earliest arcade games was Space Invaders, released in 1978. Aliens moved across the sky, and the player fired missiles up at them to try to stop the aliens from landing.

Adventure

Created for the Atari 2600 in 1979, *Adventure* allowed the player to fight dragons and hunt treasure. It was the first game to feature an Easter Egg – a hidden secret added by the programmer.

ZORK I

Some early games had no graphics. Instead, players read descriptions and typed in commands. *Zork I*, released in 1977, was one of the most popular text-adventure games. Players explored tunnels beneath a house, fighting monsters and trying to survive.

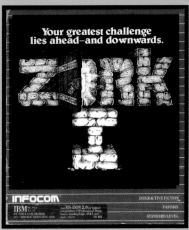

Zork 1 cover art

PAC-MAN

In this game from 1980, players used a joystick to direct *Pac-Man*, a small yellow circle, around a maze. *Pac-Man* ate dots to get points and had to avoid being eaten by four ghosts that chased him.

© 1980 BANDAI NAMCO Entertainment Inc.

NINTENDO NES

In the mid-1980s, the Nintendo NES was the most popular gaming console in the world. Its games came in plastic boxes, and players used a chunky grey controller with a handful of buttons.

Inside a computer

The physical parts of a computer are called hardware. Coders need to understand how computer hardware works so that they can write the code that tells computers what to do.

Hard drive
This is where most of the computer's data is stored.

RAM
Random Access Memory is short-term memory that stores information only when the power is on.

Storage

Computer data needs to be saved so that it can be shared and used again. This is done using storage. Today, we save data using "clouds", a form of Internet storage. Here are some physical storage devices, some of which we still use.

Punched tape
Early computers in the 1950s and 60s stored data as holes on punched tape.

Floppy disk
From the 1970s, data was stored on thin discs protected by plastic covers.

Screen
Text and images are displayed here.

Motherboard
This large circuit board holds the processor. Everything connects to it, so that different parts of the computer can communicate.

Processor
This is the "brain" of the computer. It performs most of the calculations that make the computer work.

Battery
Computers need power to work. The battery powers a laptop when it is not plugged in.

CD
A CD uses a laser to write data onto a disc. It can store much more data than a floppy disk.

DVD
DVDs have better sound and more space than CDs, so are used to store video files.

USBs are smaller than other storage devices, but can hold much more data.

USB
Memory sticks hold more data than DVDs. They plug straight into a computer.

Programma 101

In 1965, the Italian company, Olivetti, made history by creating the world's first personal desktop computer, Programma 101. This groundbreaking piece of technology was designed to work out complicated maths calculations. It was easy to use and could fit comfortably on a desk.

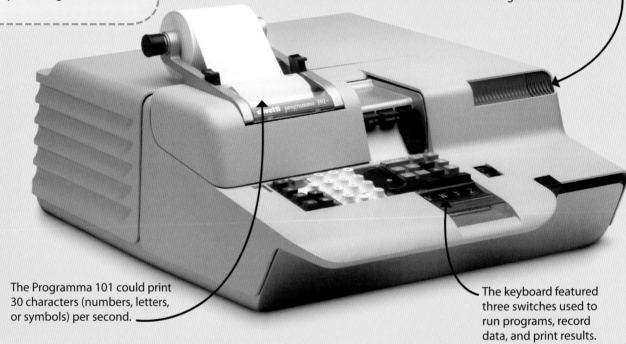

The blue light meant the machine was running and ready for input, while the red light indicated an error.

The Programma 101 could print 30 characters (numbers, letters, or symbols) per second.

The keyboard featured three switches used to run programs, record data, and print results.

Then and now

Computers have changed a lot over the years. Early computers were large enough to fill whole rooms, but modern computers are small enough to fit into a backpack. By the 1960s, people were able to buy their own personal computer for their home.

The display screen is clear and sharp, allowing users to view and edit images, create documents, play games, and access the Internet.

A handheld, movable device called a mouse is used to move around the screen.

Data that is typed on the keyboard appears immediately on the display screen.

FACT FILE

» **Weight:** 10 kg (22 lbs)

» **Function:** Data processing, information storage, and data output

» **Speed:** Almost instant results for complex functions

» **Hardware:** Keyboard with 102 keys, display screen, and microprocessor technology

Modern machine

Compared to the Programma 101, modern computers are much lighter and have a wider range of functions. These devices can be used at home and some can also be used on the move. Modern computers use smaller processors, called microprocessors, to store, process, and display huge amounts of data.

Talk like a computer

The English language has 26 letters in its alphabet, but computers and other digital devices only "speak" in 0s and 1s. Can you imagine having to talk to a friend using only 0s and 1s?

Binary
All computers communicate using two values called binary. "1" means a signal is "on" and "0" means the signal is "off". Think of a light switch; by turning the light on, you can send the message "1" to a friend in the distance, while off sends the message "0".

Bytes
A byte of data is made up of eight bits. Each bit is a 0 or 1. One byte of data can represent one of 255 different letters, numbers, or symbols.

Bits
A single bit is a 0 or 1.

Byte
Eight bits are grouped together to create one byte of data, which translates to a letter, number, or symbol. This is A.

0 1 0 0 0 0 0 1

Communication

The devices that make up a computer all communicate in binary by moving bytes of data. Everything they "say" to each other is made up of a string of 0s and 1s.

Hard drive
The hard drive is the main storage area for billions of 0s and 1s. This stores the bytes even while the computer is off.

All data stored is a series of electrical pulses that are either on, "1" or off, "0".

Bytes of data move back and forth constantly.

RAM
RAM means Random Access Memory. Bytes of data are stored here while the computer is on. The data is lost if the user has not saved it.

Processor
The central processing unit (CPU) is the "brain" of a computer, sending and receiving bytes of data. This carries out calculations and instructions.

STORING DATA

How many bytes?

Computer storage is described using bytes. These units show how many 0s and 1s the computer has space for.

1	**1 Kilobyte** is 1,024 bytes	
2	**1 Megabyte** is 1,024 kilobytes	
3	**1 Gigabyte** is 1,024 megabytes	
4	**1 Terabyte** is 1,024 gigabytes	
5	**1 Petabyte** is 1,024 terabytes	
6	**1 Exabyte** is 1,024 petabytes	

ASCII

To turn binary numbers into characters people recognise, computers use ASCII ("askey"), the American Standard Code for Information Interchange. Each set of eight binary numbers represents a number, letter, or symbol in ASCII code.

Binary	ASCII
01000001	A
01000010	B
01000011	C
00110001	1
00110010	2
00110011	3
00101110	.
00100001	!
00111111	?
01000000	@

Computer languages

A programming language is a set of instructions that tell a computer what to do. Hundreds of languages have been made for different types of programs. The six bubbles of code below all tell a computer how to say "Hello, World!". Can you match each one with its language, using the clues to help?

1

```
#include <stdio.h>
main()
{
        printf("Hello, World!");

}
```

2

```
10 PRINT "Hello, World!"
20 GOTO 10
```

3

```
print("Hello, World!")
```

A

Java
Released in 1994, Java allows a program to run on multiple operating systems without any changes to the code.

Clue:
The Java program begins with the word "class".

B

Python
A recent language that is popular with coders. Python code is short and simple. This makes it easy to learn.

Clue:
Python is the easiest and shortest code to read.

C

PHP
PHP is mainly used by coders working with web design and HTML (Hypertext Markup Language).

Clue:
The name of the language is in the actual code.

Ook!

Ook! is a programming language that was created as a joke by David Morgan-Mar. Not intended for serious use, the instructions have been changed into Orangutan words. These are "Ook.", "Ook!", and "Ook?". They can be put together to make commands.

```
Ook. Ook? Ook. Ook. Ook. Ook. Ook. Ook. Ook. Ook. Ook. Ook. Ook. Ook.
Ook. Ook.Ook. Ook. Ook. Ook. Ook! Ook? Ook? Ook. Ook. Ook. Ook. Ook.
Ook. Ook. Ook. Ook.Ook. Ook. Ook. Ook. Ook. Ook. Ook. Ook. Ook. Ook?
Ook! Ook! Ook? Ook! Ook? Ook.Ook! Ook. Ook. Ook? Ook. Ook. Ook. Ook.
Ook. Ook. Ook. Ook. Ook. Ook. Ook. Ook.Ook. Ook. Ook! Ook? Ook? Ook.
Ook. Ook. Ook. Ook. Ook. Ook. Ook. Ook. Ook?Ook! Ook! Ook? Ook!
Ook? Ook. Ook. Ook. Ook! Ook. Ook. Ook. Ook. Ook. Ook. Ook.Ook. Ook.
Ook. Ook. Ook. Ook. Ook. Ook! Ook. Ook! Ook. "Ook. Ook. Ook. Ook.
Ook. Ook. Ook! Ook. Ook. Ook? Ook. Ook? Ook. Ook? Ook. Ook. Ook.
Ook. Ook. Ook.Ook. Ook. Ook. Ook. Ook. Ook. Ook. Ook. Ook. Ook!
```

Computer code in Ook! language

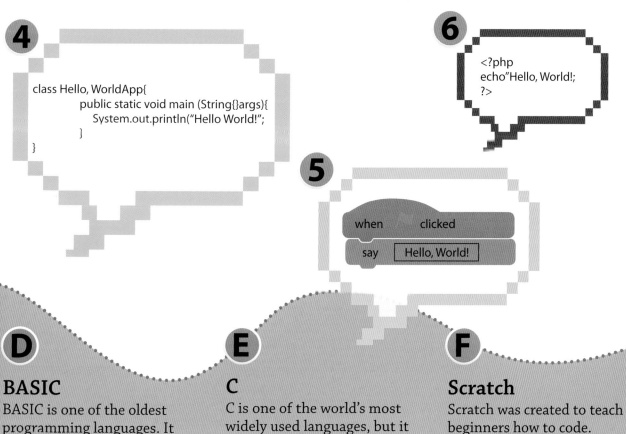

4

```
class Hello, WorldApp{
        public static void main (String{}args){
            System.out.println("Hello World!";
        }
}
```

6

```
<?php
echo"Hello, World!;
?>
```

5

```
when        clicked
say      Hello, World!
```

D

BASIC
BASIC is one of the oldest programming languages. It stands for Beginner's All-Purpose Symbolic Instruction Code.

Clue:
Each line of code starts with numbers.

E

C
C is one of the world's most widely used languages, but it can be tricky to learn. It is often used to make software that needs to run fast.

Clue:
The C program starts with a hash symbol (#).

F

Scratch
Scratch was created to teach beginners how to code. Instead of typing out code, ready-made blocks are used to build instructions.

Clue:
Scratch uses coloured blocks to build code.

Programs

Whether you say program, app, or code, what you're describing is a special set of instructions called "software". Most modern devices are controlled by software. This includes mobile phones, tablets, satellites in space, cars, planes, and even robots on Mars. Software is all created by programmers, who are also known as coders.

Mobile apps

Each app on a phone or tablet is a tiny program that works by itself. Apps can do all sorts of things. They let you take photos, send messages, and play music and games.

Drones

Drones are devices that do not need a pilot to make them fly. Instead, a person uses a remote control and special software. They are used to take photos and videos.

From coder to user

There's more to apps than just code. Coders spend a lot of time making their apps work smoothly, but they need to get the app out to all the people who might use it. Someone has to create instructions for using the app. Sometimes the app needs some help in the forms of advertising and marketing, and word of mouth is a great way to do this. Sharing and talking about the app means that it can get a lot more users, and could even go viral. This means that it has been spoken about and shared between many people.

There's an app for that!

Surgical robots

Some surgeons rely on robots to help with the most delicate operations. The robot has special code for each of its arms that help the surgeon with important tasks.

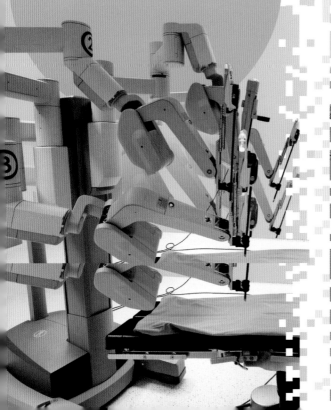

Mars Rover

The Mars Exploration Rover B is exploring the surface of Mars. It uses special code that allows it to work over 225 million km (140 million miles) away from Earth.

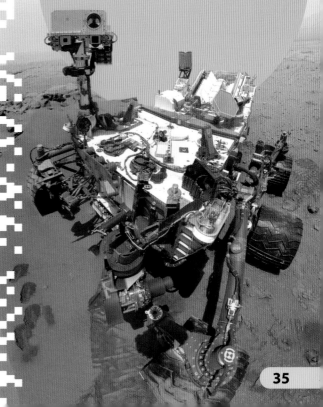

Worms and bugs

Computers don't always run smoothly. Some people spread bad code, such as worms, to damage or steal information on a computer. Programs may also stop working if there are errors in the code. These are called bugs. Anti-virus programs and "firewalls" are software that can protect computers from bad code.

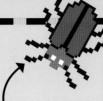

Computer errors have been called bugs since 1945, when a university computer in the USA was found to have a moth inside it.

Computer hackers

Hackers are people who write bad programs, called malware, to gain illegal access to a computer. They can then steal information, like passwords or personal details. They can also damage or delete important data on the computer.

Trojan horse

A Trojan horse is a file that pretends to be harmless. Once opened, however, it loads a program that takes control of your computer.

Computer virus

A virus is a type of malware that attaches itself to a program on a computer and runs automatically, destroying files.

Backdoor programs

Backdoor programs ignore your computer's normal security and allow hackers to break in without a password.

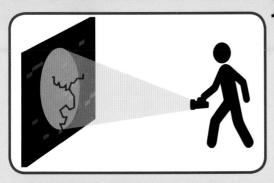

Vulnerability scanners

Hackers use programs called vulnerability scanners to look for weaknesses in a computer's "firewall" (protection) system.

Sniffers

Sniffers monitor information travelling over a computer network. They capture the passwords and user IDs of anyone using the network.

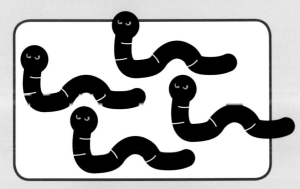

Computer worms

Computer worms infect networks by sending copies of themselves to all the machines in the system. They are harder to stop than viruses because they do not have to attach themselves to a program.

Keylogging

Keylogging lets hackers monitor every key that is pressed on someone's keyboard without them knowing. This lets them see the user's passwords or other private information.

Bugs

A bug is a mistake or fault found in a computer program or system. Bugs can cause a program to run incorrectly – for example, by showing strange text or objects on the screen. They can also cause a program to stop working completely.

```
switch (i) {
  case 1:
    do_something(1); break;
  case 2:
    do_something(2); break;
  case 3:
    do_something(1); break;
  case 4:
    do_something(4); break;
  default:
    break;
}
```

This is an error in the code – a bug. Case 1 has incorrectly been copied under case 3.

The Internet

The Internet is a network that links together computers all over the world. It was first thought of in the 1960s, but was only used by a handful of people in universities. Now, millions of people use it every day, to communicate with each other, to find things out, and for entertainment. It lets us do many things quickly and easily that would otherwise take much longer.

Slow information

We use the Internet to find things out almost instantly. Without it we would have to find a book about what we wanted to know, and then look it up, which would take a lot longer.

Snail mail

We send around 2.4 million emails every second. To send that many messages by post would cost about £132 million ($165 million), and the letters would take several days to arrive!

Map reading

Mobile phones use satellites in space to show positions on maps. Without the Internet, phones would not be in touch with satellites, so wouldn't be able to show you where you are.

Sending files

The Internet lets us share and download files instantly. Without it we could only share using wires between computers or by putting copies in the post.

Social not working

Social networking apps let you talk with your friends all the time.

You can chat, arrange to meet up, and share the latest news with large groups of friends at once.

Shopping

You can buy almost anything you want using the Internet, from food and drink to giant plastic elephants! Everything is put in the post to you, so you don't have to go to the shops.

What to watch?

The Internet lets us watch films instantly. We can download whatever we want at the click of a button instead of having to find and watch DVDs.

What is an app?

Apps are sets of instructions written in code. They are mostly used on phones and tablets, to do lots of different things, from playing games to making video calls. There are plenty of apps designed especially for kids.

Gaming
Quizzes, races, and puzzles are all fun, popular types of game apps. Some are free, but others charge money for things within the game, so be careful!

Shopping
Shopping apps let people buy things without leaving the house. Most big shops have apps. You can also bid against other people to buy things in auctions.

App building

Apps on your phone or computer don't just appear fully formed. It takes a lot of work to get them from a first idea to a finished program. Here's how it's done.

Idea
People have ideas for new apps. These apps often try to do something useful, for which an app doesn't already exist.

Design
The look of an app and how people use it is important. Popular apps usually look good and are easy to use.

Smartphones

Smartphones are mini computers that you can carry around. Unlike a desktop computer, they are small enough to use on the go. Smartphones have an operating system. This is a built-in set of instructions that lets apps work. Apple's iOS and Google's Android are the two most popular operating systems.

Smartphones in action

Maps

These apps use the Internet to pinpoint your location on a map. They can show you where you are, and help you find where you want to go quickly and easily.

Communication

Phones aren't just for making calls. Apps let people talk in lots of different ways, including using video calls, picture messages, and group chats.

Programming
Every app is made up of code. The code is tested many times before the app is released, to make sure it works properly.

Feedback
Once the app is in use, people give feedback about what does and doesn't work. Programmers tweak the code until it works perfectly.

! WOW!

In 2016, over **two million** apps were available for **smartphones.**

Everyday coding

Although we can't see them, codes are all around us, helping us every day. Computers use code to make modern technology run smoothly. Here are some examples of coding in everyday life.

Traffic lights

Coding is used to control the flow of traffic in many towns and cities. A computer sends coded instructions to the traffic lights to tell them when to change colour. Drivers and people on foot then know when to stop and when to go.

Computer games

Computer games can take players to imaginary worlds. Every game has code working behind the scenes that becomes instructions to make your character jump high or your car go faster.

Vending machines

After you have inserted money and made your selection from a vending machine, the code will work out how much change you need, and then drop your item down to a tray for you to pick up.

Microwaves

Simple coded instructions control the timer on your microwave and the temperature your food is cooked at. The code starts working when you press the buttons on the microwave.

Barcode scanner

Every item in a shop has a unique code of lines to identify it. These lines, or barcodes, are read by a computer that finds the item and its price in a database so you can buy it.

Beep!

Car dashboard

Vehicles

Cars use computer code to monitor their engines and make sure they run properly. Code also controls things like the indicators on the dashboard and windscreen wipers.

Calculator

Calculators use code to work out the answers to mathematical questions. They display the results immediately on the screen.

Smartboard

These giant screens use computer coded instructions to let students choose and control what information is shown. All they have to do is touch the screen.

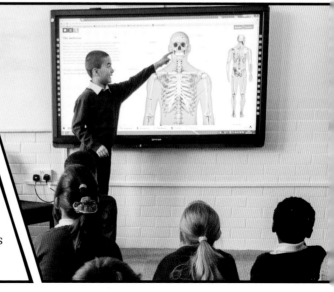

Scratch

One of the easiest programming languages to learn is Scratch. Programs are made by joining together coloured blocks that tell characters on screen what to do. Scratch lets you make your own stories, games, music, and art.

Scratch layout

The screen layout has space for your instructions on the right. On the left is the "stage", where your code is put into action.

This is the stage, where you will see what you create.

The blocks of instructions are called scripts.

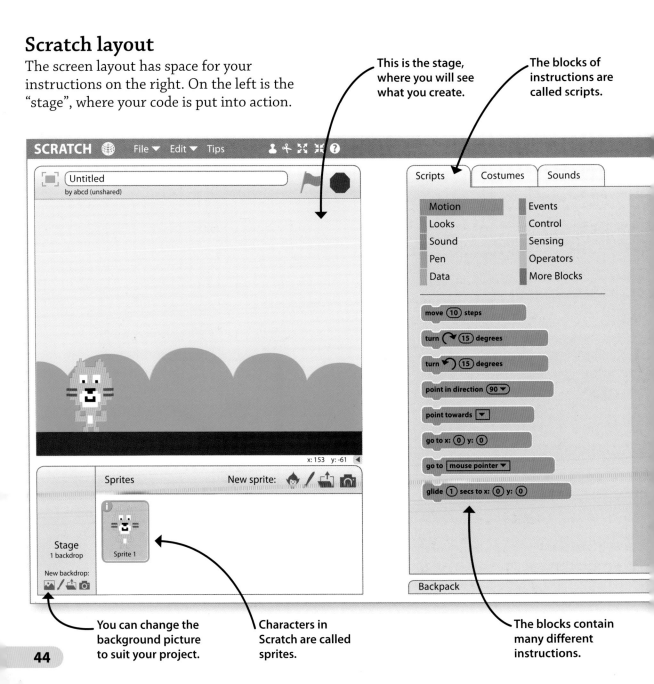

You can change the background picture to suit your project.

Characters in Scratch are called sprites.

The blocks contain many different instructions.

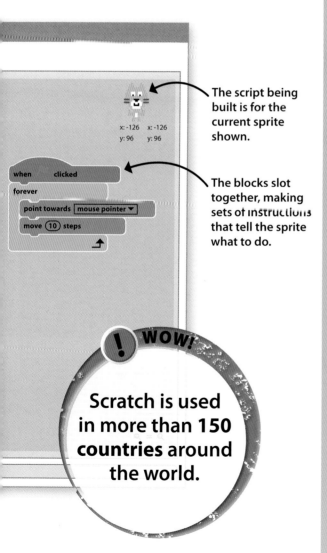

The script being built is for the current sprite shown.

x: -126   x: -126
y: 96   y: 96

when   clicked

forever

point towards mouse pointer ▼

move 10 steps

The blocks slot together, making sets of instructions that tell the sprite what to do.

! WOW!

Scratch is used in more than 150 countries around the world.

Sprites

Sprites are the characters that are used in Scratch. They are controlled by coded sets of instructions called scripts. Sprites can move around, talk in speech bubbles, and appear and disappear.

Draw your own sprites
Scratch has many sprites that you can choose from. There's also a drawing tool so you can create your own.

Sword moves down.

Leg moves out.

Pirate costume 1
Costumes are pictures of sprites in different poses. Swapping costumes can make this pirate move.

Pirate costume 2
When switching from costume 1 to costume 2, the pirate's leg and sword appear to move.

Raspberry Pi

The Raspberry Pi is a mini-computer, made to teach people how computers work. It connects to all kinds of devices, such as TVs, cameras, and even robots, and has enough power to run similar programs to a full-sized computer.

Micro SD card

A tiny memory card stores the operating system, programs, and data.

Connector for LCD display panel

A liquid crystal display (LCD) panel can be connected to this port.

HDMI video

A computer screen or modern television can be connected to this port.

Camera port

Attaching a camera lets the Pi take photos and videos.

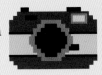

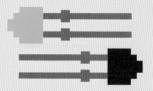

GPIO pins

Lights or buzzers can be attached to these pins. They light up or sound when the Pi is in use.

USB ports

A mouse and keyboard can be connected to these ports for use with a computer screen.

LAN port

The Raspberry Pi can access the Internet with a wired connection using this port.

WOW!

More than **11 million** Raspberry Pis have been sold since its release in **2012**.

Audio output

Headphones or speakers can be connected here for listening to music.

Key coders

Computing has changed a lot since the first computers were invented, and programmers across the globe are working on new technology all the time. Some people create things that change our world. How many of these famous coders do you know about?

TIM BERNERS-LEE

English computer programmer Tim Berners-Lee created the World Wide Web in 1989. The World Wide Web links Internet web pages together, and is now used by millions of people across the globe.

GRACE HOPPER

A Rear Admiral in the US Navy as well as a computer scientist, Grace Hopper created the world's first computer compiler – a program that converts ordinary language into code that a computer can understand.

MARK ZUCKERBERG

University student Mark Zuckerberg became one of the youngest billionaires in the world when he created social media website Facebook in 2004. The site had one million users within ten months.

MARGARET HAMILTON

American computer programmer Margaret Hamilton worked for the US space agency, NASA. She was responsible for developing the on-board flight software that landed the first people on the Moon in 1969.

STEVE JOBS AND STEVE WOZNIAK

Founders of technology company Apple, Americans Steve Jobs and Steve Wozniak built one of the earliest home computers in 1976. Now the Apple brand is one of the most successful in the world.

BILL GATES

American Bill Gates co-founded Microsoft, a computer software company, in 1975. Ten years later, Microsoft created Windows, now the most widely used operating system in the world.

SERGEY BRIN AND LARRY PAGE

Google, the world's most popular search engine, was created by Sergey Brin and Larry Page in 1998. Today, around 80 to 85 per cent of all Internet queries are typed into Google's search engine.

Meet the expert

Coder and author Jeff Atwood co-created Stack Overflow, a website for answering questions about coding, and Discourse, a program for communicating online.

Q: We know it is something to do with coding, but what is your actual job?

A: My job is to write commands that tell the computer what to do, and to give it commands that make it do a better job.

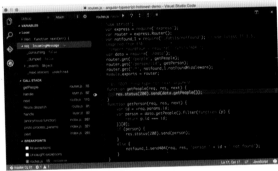

Code on screen

Q: What made you decide to become a software developer?

A: I've always loved computers and computer games, and once I saw that I could build my own games – not just play games other people create – I was hooked.

Q: Do you have a favourite thing that you have developed?

A: We built Stack Overflow, which is like a Wikipedia for programmers!

Q: Do you use any special equipment?

A: We use fast computers, with lots of memory. We also use multiple monitors and nice chairs.

Q: What do you love most about coding?

A: Software is easy to change to make it better, and software can also encourage people to do better things and help others.

Q: What is a usual work day for you?

A: I work from home, so I get up and head to my home office. I talk to my team via the Internet.

Q: What are the best and worst things about your job?

A: The best thing about my job is that software can touch so many people – through their smartphones, through their laptops and computers. The worst thing about my job is that I spend a lot of time talking to the computer. It can be unforgiving when you make mistakes, even tiny ones!

Jeff's computer set-up

Meet the expert

We met computer scientist Kiki Prottsman to find out how to think like a coder. She is the curriculum manager at code.org, which aims to get more people involved in coding.

Q: We know it is something to do with coding, but what is your actual job?

A: I travel all over the place, showing students and teachers how to think like a computer scientist.

Q: What made you decide to become a computer scientist?

A: My dad taught me to program when I was a little girl. I enjoy the problem solving and creativity of computer science.

Teaching children to code

Q: Do you have a favourite thing that you have worked on?

A: The project that I'm working on right now teaches computer science using books, games, and craft projects. It's a new way of introducing kids to coding.

Dot and Dash robots

Q: Do you use any special equipment?

A: I get to play with computers, tablets, 3D printers, learning games, and robots like Dot and Dash!

Q: What do you love most about coding?

A: Computer science is a lot like ballet, poetry, or painting. It takes practice, but it's a wonderful way to express yourself.

Q: What is a usual work day for you?

A: I don't really have a usual work day. I work from home a lot, so a lot of my work happens in my pyjamas!

Q: What are the best and worst things about your job?

A: The best thing about my job is that I'm always working on something new. The worst thing is that technology and education move at very different speeds. Technology changes all the time! Schools change very slowly.

Gaming

Although they were once a rare hobby, people now spend more money on video games than music or films. They can be played on your own, or together with friends, and range from fast-paced action games to story-focused roleplaying games.

! WOW!

Tetris is the **most popular** video game ever, with **500 million** copies sold.

Competition is fierce between different brands of console

Games console

Video game consoles like Xbox or PlayStation are also computers, but their hardware is dedicated to playing games. This allows them to offer advanced graphics and sound. They become more powerful each year.

Mobile gaming

Games consoles get smaller all the time. Games that used to be too advanced for a computer can now be played, often for free, on phones or tablets. Some even use cameras to set the game in the world around the player.

Mobile phones let you play games wherever you are

Online gaming

Early computer games had only one player. These days, online gaming means millions of people can play together in "massively multiplayer" games, or share their gaming experience online. Some famous gamers attract an audience of millions.

Online gaming means you can play with people all over the world

A quitar controller helps gamers rock out in rhythm games

Special controls

Not all game controllers use buttons. Some look like instruments, dance mats, or even steering wheels. Motion controls allow gamers to play without a controller at all, as the game "watches" the player and responds to their movements.

Virtual reality

The next big step in gaming is virtual reality. A headset can surround players with lifelike graphics that respond to their movements, so they feel like they are inside the game.

Virtual reality games put players in the driver's seat

Teamwork

Many coders work in teams. Teams are useful for dividing up work, coming up with new ideas, and solving problems. A coder may be given a job due to special skills they bring to the team. Teams are also a great way for coders to share their knowledge and learn new skills.

Graphic coders

Today's apps are colourful and eye-catching with incredible details. Graphic coders work on apps, as they are skilled in areas such as font design, movement (for games), and making art.

Graphic coders receive instructions and feedback on their designs from application coders.

Application coders advise system coders of any problems with the way the apps run by talking to the customers who use them.

Application coders

One or more coders are usually in charge of creating the look of an app, and how people use it. These application coders often work closely with customers to make sure an app gives them what they want.

Web coders

Websites generally have code running behind the scenes that controls things like online payments and video loading. Web coders create this code. It is used by millions of Internet users every day.

Code for a website is often built based on design requests from application coders.

Game coders

Games are one of the most popular types of app, and entire teams consist of coders who understand how to create the special code for things like scoring, levels, and explosions.

System coders

Mobile phones, tablets, and computers run software that allows apps to communicate with them. System coders regularly have to create code so that apps can run on each different operating system.

Game coders use application coding when designing how the game will look and how players will use it.

Web coders often need special code made by system coders for different web browsers.

Game coders need to understand audio coding in order to create the sounds in games.

Audio coders

Sound is important for many types of app, especially games. Audio coders create code for the sounds you hear when you are using an app.

Learning to code

You can use books or online videos to get you started with coding. The most important thing is to code as much as you can – practice makes perfect. Code won't always be right the first time. It takes a lot of problem solving, but it is exciting when you get it right and your code works.

Coding programs

Simple programs, like Scratch, let you practise writing basic code. For example, you might write instructions that move a character round the screen.

Play!

Using coding games to learn is a great way to start coding. This is because you can work at your own pace. You can choose easy or difficult games that let you learn as much as you want.

Keyboard

Hard drive saves data to a disk, and can read data stored on disks.

Memory stores information

Build your own computer

Building a computer teaches you what the different parts are and how they work together. It's not as hard as you might think!

Mouse

Speak Code

There are many different coding languages, such as Python, Ruby, and C++. Learn as many as you can so you can write code for different things.

Code together

You don't have to learn coding by yourself. It is taught in schools all over the world. One of the most fun ways to code is with a partner or as a member of a team. Once you know your stuff, you could even teach someone else to code.

Be a robot master

Robot kits let you build a robot quite easily. You can then tell the robot what to do by writing instructions in code.

Motherboard connects different parts of the computer.

You can use code to control a robot car.

Coding facts and figures

Coding is a fascinating area to explore. Here are some weird and wonderful facts and figures you may not know about it.

HALO

GUDE

ADA

In **1980,** the American Department of Defense named a new computer language **ADA,** after the first computer programmer.

If coding was a country, the people living there would speak the **third highest number of languages** in the world, after the people in Indonesia and Papua New Guinea.

010101010
101010101

The world's **youngest computer programmer** qualified as a Microsoft Office professional **at age 6!**

£2,239

($2,841) is how much the Apple 1, released in July 1976, would cost today. Modern Apple Macs start at around £1,025 ($1,300).

Apple 1

Modern Apple Mac

The first known use of the word **computer** was in a book in **1613**.

It meant a person who carried out calculations.

The first **computer virus** created outside of a lab was written as a joke by a **15-year-old student!**

35 is the number of days it took the app **Angry Birds** to reach **50 million** users.

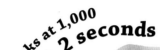

A Google search looks at 1,000 **computers in 0.2 seconds**

The fastest computer in the world is the **Sunway TaihuLight**. It can do **39 quadrillion calculations per second!**

10 Colossus machines were used at Bletchley Park in Milton Keynes to help crack German codes during World War II.

200 is the number of hours it took to create *Spacewar*, one of the first video games.

11 kg The first laptop computer weighed 11 kg (24 lb). That's the same as an 18-month-old child!

Glossary

Here are the meanings of some words that are useful for you to know when learning all about coding.

algorithm Set of simple step-by-step instructions for performing a task. An algorithm written for computers is called a program

app Programs designed to be used for a specific task, usually on mobile devices

application *see* app

ASCII Code for storing numbers and letters in a format computers can understand

assembly code Simple computer code that is not easily read by humans

back end Parts of a computer program that are hidden from the user

binary Code used for storing information on computers. It uses only two digits, 0 and 1, to represent letters and numbers

bit Smallest unit of data in a computer. Computer data is stored in bytes; one byte is eight bits

browser Program used to access the Internet

bug Mistake in a program, which makes it behave incorrectly or stop working

chip Tiny device that stores memory or runs programs

code Written commands, or language, used in a computer program

A screen is part of a computer's **hardware**.

computers Machines that can perform different tasks by following programs

console Computer designed for playing video games

data Another word for information. Data is measured in bits, and stored in a computer's memory

debug To check code for errors, and remove them

digital Any electronic device that uses binary code

download Receiving a copy of data from one computer to another over the Internet

encryption Converting computer data to another form to keep it secret so only certain people can read it

graphics Images created by a computer

hackers People who write bad programs, called malware, to gain illegal access to a computer

hard drive In-built device for storing information permanently on a computer

hardware Physical parts of a computer, like keyboards and cables

HTML Language used for programming webpages. It stands for Hypertext Markup Language

Internet Network that links computers across the world

language Set of words and rules used to give computers instructions

malware Harmful programs that steal information or damage computers

memory Physical device on a computer used for storing information immediately

motherboard Printed circuit board that connects all the main parts of a computer, and passes instructions between them

network Two or more linked computers that communicate electronically with each other

operating system Most important program on a computer. It controls all the functions of the computer

processor Computer chip that runs programs by following machine code

program Set of instructions a computer follows to complete a task

programming Creating instructions for a computer to follow, written in a special language

RAM Computer's short-term memory, used to help it run faster. RAM stands for Random Access Memory

Raspberry Pi Tiny computer used to help teach people how computers work. It connects to different devices and can run programs

ROM Computer's long-term memory, which stores the important programs that tell it how to work. ROM stands for Read-Only Memory

runtime Time during which a program is working, or running. A fast computer has a low runtime

Scratch One of the easiest programming languages to learn. Coloured blocks are used to program and animate characters

server Computer that can transfer information between computers over a network connection

social media Website or application that allows users to communicate and share content with each other

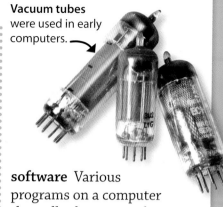

Vacuum tubes were used in early computers.

software Various programs on a computer that tell it how to work

upload Sending a copy of data to another computer over the Internet

vacuum tubes Glass tubes used in early computers as on-off switches

virus Malware that attaches itself to another program and destroys files

website Collection of linked webpages on the Internet

Wi-Fi Technology that allows computers to connect to other electronic devices or the Internet without using wires

World Wide Web Collection of pages of information, called webpages, which link to each other like a web

worm Harmful program that copies itself to other computers

Index

Acknowledgements

The publisher would like to thank the following people for their assistance in the preparation of this book: Dan Crisp for illustrations; Caroline Hunt for proofreading; Hilary Bird for compiling the index; and Jeff Atwood and Kiki Prottsman for their "Meet the expert" interviews. Scratch is developed by the lifelong Kindergarten Group at MIT Media Lab. See **http://scratch.mit.edu**

The publisher would like to thank the following for their kind permission to reproduce their photographs:

(Key: a-above; b-below/bottom; c-centre; f-far; l-left; r-right; t-top)

2 123RF.com: Сергей Тряпицын (fbl, bc). **Bridgeman Images:** Private Collection / Prismatic Pictures (br). **Digital Vision:** Don Farrall (cb). **Dreamstime.com:** Alisali (bl). **3 123RF.com:** golubovy (bc). **Dreamstime. com:** Jannoon028 (bl). **Getty Images:** Mary Delaney Cooke (crb). **4 Alamy Stock Photo:** Ievgen Chepil (tl); Artur Marciniec (bc); Nippon News (cr). **5 Alamy Stock Photo:** Blue Jean Images (tl). **Getty Images:** Bloomberg (cb). **NASA:** (cr). **6 Alamy Stock Photo:** Wil Davis (clb). **Dorling Kindersley:** British Museum (br). **7 Alamy Stock Photo:** Monika Wisniewska (bl). **8-9 Alamy Stock Photo:** Photo Researchers (tc). **Getty Images:** Education Images (bc). **8 Getty Images:** Science & Society Picture Library (bl). **9 Alamy Stock Photo:** Photo Researchers (tr). **Getty Images:** C Squared Studios (br). **10-11 Alamy Stock Photo:** Pictorial Press (bc). **11 Dreamstime.com:** Andersastphoto / MacBook Air® is a trademark of Apple Inc., registered in the U.S. and other countries. (br). **Getty Images:** Science & Society Picture Library (c). **13 Rex by Shutterstock:** Eileen Tweedy (bl). **14 Alamy Stock Photo:** Interfoto (tr). **16-17 Alamy Stock Photo:** Roger Bacon (tc). **Bridgeman Images:** Private Collection / Prismatic Pictures (bc). **18-19 Getty Images:** Mary Delaney Cooke. **19 Alamy Stock Photo:** Pictorial Press (tb). **Rex by Shutterstock:** Reativ Studio Heinemann / Imagebroker (cra). **20 Alamy Stock Photo:** Zoonar / Peter Schmalfeldt (b). **21 Alamy Stock Photo:** Mark Waugh (tr). **Science Photo Library:** Andy Bernhaut (br); Earl Scott (c). **24 Alamy Stock Photo:** Interfoto (cra); Sinibomb Images (bl, fbl). **©TAITO CORPORATION 1978 ALL RIGHTS RESERVED:** (br). **25 © 1980 BANDAI NAMCO Entertainment Inc.:** (bl). **Alamy Stock Photo:** Interfoto / History (cra). **Getty Images:** GamesMaster Magazine (br). **26-27 Dreamstime.com:** Rawgrouppro (tc). **26 Dreamstime.com:** Alisali (bc). **27 Digital Vision:** Don Farrall (br). **28 Photo Scala, Florence:** The Museum of Modern Art, New York (c). **29 Alamy Stock Photo:** A. Astes / iMac® is a trademark of Apple Inc., registered in the U.S. and other countries. (cb). **Dreamstime.com:** Anton Samsonov / iMac® is a trademark of Apple Inc., registered in the U.S. and other countries. (t). **34 Dreamstime.com:** Jannoon028 (bl); Tyler Olson (br). **35 Alamy Stock Photo:** Javier Larrea (bl). **Dreamstime.com:** Jirsa (tr); Syda Productions (tr/image on Hoading). **NASA:** JPL-Caltech / Malin Space Science Systems (br). **38 Dreamstime.com:** Luminis (clb); Vitaliy Tsvetkov (clb/bacground books); Photographerlondon (br). **39 Alamy Stock Photo:** D. Hurst (bc). **41 Alamy Stock Photo:** Leland Bobbe (tr). **42 Alamy Stock Photo:** B Christopher (bl); Cigdem Simsek (cr). **Dorling Kindersley:** Ruth Jenkinson (crb). **43 Alamy Stock Photo:** National Motor Museum (tc). **iStockphoto.com:** erzetic (tl). **47 Getty Images:** Yoshikazu Tsuno (cra). **48 Alamy Stock Photo:** European Pressphoto Agency B.v. (tr). **Getty Images:** ynthia Johnson (clb). **Rex by Shutterstock:** John Salangsang (crb). **49 Alamy Stock Photo:** Roger Bacon (tr); ES Imagery (clb); European Pressphoto Agency B.v. (crb). NASA. **50 Jeff Atwood:** (tr). **51 Kiki Prottsman:** (tr). **Wonder Workshop:** Kiki Prottsman (cra). **52 Dreamstime.com:** Lisa F. Young (cl); **Getty Images:** Ruslan Shamukov (br). **53 Getty Images:** Bloomberg (tr); Amy Graves (cl); Rosdiana Ciaravolo (br). **56 123RF.com:** Сергей Тряпицын (clb, bc, br). **57 123RF.com:** golubovy (br); Сергей Тряпицын (bl). **Alamy Stock Photo:** Ron Nickel (cra). **58 Alamy Stock Photo:** A. Astes / iMac® is a trademark of Apple Inc., registered in the U.S. and other countries. (br); IanDagnall Computing (tr). **Dreamstime.com:** Anton Samsonov / iMac® is a trademark of Apple Inc., registered in the U.S. and other countries. (crb). **Science Photo Library:** Volker Steger (bc). **59 Alamy Stock Photo:** Xinhua (cb). **Dreamstime.com:** Lim Seng Kui (c). **60 Dreamstime.com:** Andersastphoto / MacBook Air® is a trademark of Apple Inc., registered in the U.S. and other countries. (bl). **Getty Images:** Science & Society Picture Library (tl). **61 Rex by Shutterstock:** Reativ Studio Heinemann / Imagebroker (tr). **62 Alamy Stock Photo:** Nippon News (tl)

Cover images: *Front:* **123RF.com:** golubovy ca; **Bridgeman Images:** Private Collection / Prismatic Pictures br; **Dreamstime.com:** Alisali crb; **Rex by Shutterstock:** Eileen Tweedy cra; **Photo Scala, Florence:** The Museum of Modern Art, New York cr; *Back:* **Alamy Stock Photo:** Nippon News tr; **Dreamstime.com:** Tyler Olson clb; *Front Flap:* **123RF.com:** Сергей Тряпицын tl, tr/ (mother borad); **Alamy Stock Photo:** A. Astes / iMac® is a trademark of Apple Inc., registered in the U.S. and other countries. br; **Rex by Shutterstock:** Reativ Studio Heinemann / Imagebroker cr; *Back Flap:* **Getty Images:** Nash Photos clb; **iStockphoto.com:** Naumoid tc; *Front Endpapers:* **123RF.com:** Alexmillos 0crb; **Alamy Stock Photo:** Interfoto / History 0bc (Apple Lisa), Interfoto / Personalities 0cla, Photo Researchers 0bc, World History Archive 0bl; **Getty Images:** Bettmann 0ca, Miguel Riopa 0ca (Ray Tomlinson); *Back Endpapers:* **Alamy Stock Photo:** European Pressphoto Agency B.v. 0tc, 0bl, Granger, NYC 0cb (Hollerith), Photo Researchers 0ca; **Bridgeman Images:** Private Collection / Prismatic Pictures 0cb; **Getty Images:** Apic 0cb (Intel microprocessor), Freek Van Den Bergh 0br; **iStockphoto.com:** Mbbirdy / iPad® is a trademark of Apple Inc., registered in the U.S. and other countries. 0cb (I pad) b

All other images © Dorling Kindersley
For further information see:
www.dkimages.com

My Findout facts:

Computer History

Computers are machines that process information.
Discover some incredible computing inventions.

Abacus
Abacus beads are used for basic maths around the world, including in Egypt, Greece, and China.

First clock
Created in China, this mechanical clock is powered by running water.

Analytical Engine
Charles Babbage designs the Analytical Engine, an early gear-driven computer.

ENIAC
The first electronic general-purpose computer is built at the University of Pennsylvania, in the USA.

| 500 BCE | 200 BCE | 700 CE | 1801 | 1822 | 1890 | 1936 | 1943 |

Punch card loom
Joseph Jacquard invents a punch card loom that weaves stored fabric patterns.

Tabulating machine
Herman Hollerith creates a machine that uses punched cards to store data.

Antikythera
The Ancient Greeks use this device to predict the position of stars and eclipses.

The Antikythera was recovered from a shipwreck.

Turing machine
Alan Turing proposes a machine that can be programmed to follow instructions.

The Hollerith machine recorded data from the 1890 census.